How to Manage Your Time

How to Manage Your Time

Time Management Strategies for Active Christians

From the Success in Christian Living series—a practical approach to achieving your goals for time, money, motivation, and human potential.

by Dennis E. Hensley

Published by Warner Press
Anderson, Indiana

Copyright ©1989 by Warner Press, Inc.
and Dennis E. Hensley
ISBN 0-87162-474-5
All Rights Reserved
Printed in the United States of America
Warner Press, Inc.
Arlo F. Newell, Editor in Chief
Dan Harman, Book Editor
Caroline Smith, Editor

Contents

Introduction:
Redeeming the Time

Ben Franklin once wrote, "Time is the stuff of which life is made." How true. Life is nothing more than the time we have on this earth.

Time has limitations, however. It's important that we recognize that fact. Nearly two-thousand years ago the Bible noted that sooner or later everyone dies (Heb. 9:27).

We are all destined for a guaranteed termination. No one has ever beaten the system. In fact, the Bible even tells us about how long we have before our termination: **three score and ten** (Ps. 90:10). It's interesting to note that even though that calculation was recorded two millennia ago, it hasn't changed. After twenty centuries of medical, educational, social, and scientific advances, research conducted annually by insurance companies reveals that the average person lives to be from seventy to seventy-five years old (three score and ten).

Once that fact hits home with us, we begin to realize how truly important it is to redeem the limited time we do have. To waste time is to waste life. No one can afford to do that.

Every moment of life is valuable. Once time is gone, it's gone forever. You can't buy it back, borrow it back, bribe it back, or even pray it back. A wasted moment is irretrievable.

You may think you have plenty of time to accomplish everything you yet want to do. Well, what if I told you that most people spend 70 percent of each year in nonwork-related activities? That's true.

Consider for a moment the person who works a forty-hour work week. This person begins the year with 365 work days. Most workers get two weeks paid vacation, plus 50 weekends off (14 + 102 = 116 days). This leaves only 249 work days. Now, subtract time off for national holidays, sick leave, personal days, and in-house training days and you end up with only 235 days. That alone shows that 36 percent of your year is guaranteed to be **nonwork oriented** even before you begin.

Now, what about those remaining 235 days? Are they productive? Usually not. If you take a one-hour lunch break Monday through Friday, that equals 260 non-working hours per year. If you sleep eight hours per day, that adds up to 2,920 nonworking hours per year. All in all, most Americans spend about 30 percent of each year doing something productive and about 70 percent of each year in nonworking activities.

That's a hard fact to face, yet something with which we all need to come to grips. The first directive from God was to subdue the earth. You can't accomplish much subduing if seven out of every ten hours of your life are spent in nonproductive activities.

I'm convinced that the world needs more people who are time conscious. In A.D. 54 the Apostle Paul wrote that "if any would not work, neither should he eat" (2 Thess. 3:10). Fifteen centuries later Captain John Smith instituted the same rule when he and his followers set about to build a colony in New England. People who *use* the time of their lives are able to achieve incredible goals.

Time management seems such an obvious avenue to success that it's rather amazing that more people don't maximize its use. But they don't. Why, I don't know. It stands to reason that if someone only works 21 percent of a week (40 hours) and then spends 79 percent of the week (125 hours) using up the cash he or she earned in the 21 percent of the time, expenditures are obviously going to equal or exceed income.

That's surely no way to get ahead. And that's why most people *don't* get ahead in life. According to recent studies conducted by life insurance companies, success and failure rates are predictable: Take a random sample of any 100 working people in America and follow them from ages 25 through 65. By age 65 only one person will be wealthy; four people will be financially independent; five people will still be working to support themselves; 36 of the people will be dead; and the remaining 54 will be virtually penniless and in need of welfare, charities, Social Security, and relatives to support them.

How can it be that so many people failed to set goals, failed to organize their lives, failed to accept responsibility, failed to reach their potential, failed to put a value on their **life TIME?** Which statistic reflects **your** life?

The Old Testament teaches an interesting, if subtle, lesson about time management. About one year after Moses had led the Children of Israel out of Egypt and into the desert, he was instructed by God to count all the people. Surely, with worrying about hot days, cold nights, low rations, lack of water, attacks from enemies, and general organizational problems, Moses didn't need any new worries. Taking a census was the last thing on his mind.

Nevertheless, Numbers 1:1-3 says, "And the Lord spake unto Moses in the wilderness . . . on the first day of the second month, in the second year after they were come out of the land of Egypt, saying, Take ye the sum of all the congregation of the children of Israel."

We later read this interesting passage in Numbers 1:17-19: "And Moses . . . assembled all the congregation together on the first day of the second month, and . . . he numbered them in the wilderness of Sinai."

Did you follow that? Moses was already greatly burdened with problems. But when given a new challenge, he began to work on it **that very day.** He didn't waste time complaining or making excuses or setting up a committee to study the available options. He got to work. And by the end of the day, Moses had completed the job. His mission was accomplished, his task completed, his goal obtained.

Now, I challenge you to be equally as time conscious. If you want to manage time and not allow it to slip away from you, then start today. Begin to get a grip on life by mastering the lessons and systems of time management found in this book.

Your study here will be time well spent.

Part 1:

Gauging Our Time

I f we've learned anything from the wisdom accumulated over the ages, it has been this: time passes quickly.

King David wrote three thousand years ago, "You have made my days as a mere handbreadth; the span of my years is as nothing before you" (Ps. 39:5).

In other psalms we read, "They are like the new grass of morning—though in the morning it springs up new, by evening it is dry and withered. (Ps. 90:5-6).

Time goes by so quickly, we dare not squander any of it. How about you? Do you really know how you spend your days? On page 7 you'll find a twenty-question quiz titled "Managing Your Time: How Do You Rate?" Take a moment now to respond to that quiz. Find out, in all honesty, just how well or how poorly you currently are managing your time.

Chapter 1:

Time Trek

If after taking the quiz on page 7 you've discovered that you have many bad time management habits to break, don't feel alone. Most people are just like you. Fortunately, if your perspective is right, you will be able to overcome these bad habits quickly.

If you are wondering what I mean by perspective, I'm referring to the way you currently view time. Each person has his or her own way of perceiving time.

A pilot was once flying near the airport in Nashville. He called the control tower and asked, "What time is it?"

A voice responded, "That depends on which airline you're with."

"What!" said the pilot. "That's ridiculous. What difference does it make which airline I'm with? I just want to know what time it is."

"Oh, it makes a lot of difference," said the voice in the tower. "You see, if you're with United Airlines, the answer is it's zero-eight-hundred hours. If you're with Delta Airlines, the answer is it's eight o'clock in the morning. But if you're with Fred's Crop Dusting Service, the answer is, the big hand is on the twelve and the little hand is on the eight."

There it is: we all have different perspectives when it comes to viewing time. (The little anecdote "Priceless Bank Account" on page 9 may help you gain even yet another perspective on how you view time.)

Some years ago I was hired to prepare time management training materials for Dun and Bradstreet and for the New York Life Insurance Company. In the process of researching the topic, I discovered that almost no one could give me an accurate accounting of how he or she spent his or her days, weeks, or months.

If I asked people to tell me accurately how many hours they had watched television the previous week, they answered, "Gosh, I guess I really don't know." They also didn't know how many hours they had spent on the telephone, eating meals, writing reports, or amusing themselves with hobbies or activities.

To bring their week into focus for them, I developed a "Time Management Grid" (now known as the "Hensley Grid." See page 10). Each person was asked to carry the grid for seven consecutive days from 8 A.M. until 5:30 P.M. and to write down every major activity he or she did during each half-hour period.

At the end of one week, they were asked to tally the amount of organized time they spent at each activity and then to tally the amount of unorganized time. Most of the participants were shocked at what they discovered.

"Surely I didn't really spend thirty-seven hours watching TV," said one man.

"This is amazing," admitted one woman. "According to my own recordkeeping, I spent nearly eleven hours on the telephone."

"This is incredible," said a salesperson. "Last week I spent seven hours sitting in waiting rooms until my prospective clients called me in."

These were shocking, but valuable discoveries. Once these people found out **how** and **where** their time was being mismanaged, they were able to take steps to correct those situations. You can do likewise if you, too, will make use of the grid for one week.

The grid will also show you ways to overlap your time. For example, suppose at the end of the week you noticed that under Organized Time you had logged no hours for "Study" but five hours for "Travel." (The travel time was made up of a half-hour drive to work in the morning and a half-hour drive home each night.)

Noticing this, you can put a cassette tape player in the front seat of your car. Each morning from then on, you can listen to training tapes on how to speak German, how to dress for success, how to study the Bible, or any other learning experience that may interest you. You will still be logging five hours of travel time each week, but now you also will be simultaneously logging five hours of study time. The value of your time has just been doubled.

The time which we have at our disposal every day is elastic; the passions that we feel expand it, those we inspire contract it; and habit fills up what remains.

—Marcel Proust

Chapter 2:

Manage Your Time
(How Do You Rate?)

In this Chapter, you will take a hard look at how you are presently using your time. Then use the information at the end to rate yourself.

Yes	No	Do you:
___	___	1. Begin the day before planning what must get done?
___	___	2. Begin a job before thinking it through?
___	___	3. Leave jobs before they are finished?
___	___	4. Do the simple or less-important work before the more important (and possibly more unattractive) work?
___	___	5. Assign tasks without specifying quantity, quality, and time?
___	___	6. Assign difficult tasks without checking to see if the worker is in need of assistance?
___	___	7. Have trouble saying no, even though you cannot see when the task will get completed?

____	____	8. Do most of the work yourself rather than assign someone to help you?
____	____	9. Do work by hand that a machine could do?
____	____	10. Do activities or projects that aren't really part of your job?
____	____	11. Spend a lot of time doing the things you have always done and that you know you are good at doing?
____	____	12. Feel that the best ways to do things are the ways you have always done them?
____	____	13. Start projects that you have little interest in or know that you probably will not finish?
____	____	14. Make sure the short, easy tasks get done early?
____	____	15. Often operate by crisis management?
____	____	16. Try to juggle a large number of different jobs?
____	____	17. Handle the concerns of employees immediately when requested?
____	____	18. Socialize daily during business hours either in person or by telephone?
____	____	19. Get distracted while working by such things as newspapers, friends who drop in to see you, and low-priority mail?
____	____	20. Make several trips outside your office rather than group errands together for one trip?
		Now total your scores.

To rate yourself, count the number of yes answers and the number of no answers. If you answered *yes* more than *no*, you have a lot of work ahead. If you have five to ten yeses, you can improve on the effective use of your time. If you answered *yes* to more than fifteen questions you are in big trouble.

Chapter 3:

Priceless Bank Account

Suppose you had a bank that credited your account each morning with $86,400, but carried over no balance from day to day. It allowed you to keep no cash in your account. Every evening it canceled the amount you had failed to use during the day. What would you do?

Draw out every cent, of course!

Well, you have such a bank, and its name is *TIME*. Every morning it credits you with 86,400 seconds. Every night it rules off, as lost, whatever of this you have failed to invest for a good purpose.

It carries over no balances. It allows no overdrafts.

Each day it opens a new account with you.

Each night it burns the records of that day.

If you fail to use the day's deposits, the loss is yours and no one else's.

There is no drawing against the "tomorrow."

You must live in the present—on today's deposits.

Invest it to get from it the utmost in health, happiness, and success!

Author Unknown

Time Management

DAY	ACTIVITIES PERFORMED
8:00- 8:30	
9:00- 9:30	
10:00-10:30	
11:00-11:30	
12:00-12:30	
1:00- 1:30	
2:00- 2:30	
3:00- 3:30	
4:00- 4:30	
5:00- 5:30	

Activity	Amount of Time Unorganized	Amount of Time Organized
Amusement	_____	_____
Calling	_____	_____
Civic Activities	_____	_____
Eating	_____	_____
Office Work	_____	_____
Planning	_____	_____
Prospecting	_____	_____
Religious Activities	_____	_____
Sleeping	_____	_____
Studying	_____	_____
Television	_____	_____
Thinking	_____	_____
Traveling	_____	_____
Waiting	_____	_____
Writing Reports	_____	_____
Other	_____	_____
_____	_____	_____
_____	_____	_____
_____	_____	_____
_____	_____	_____

ΙΙNothing is particularly hard if you divide it into small jobs.**ΙΙ**

—Henry Ford

Chapter 4:

Career Analysis

I f poor time-management skills have kept you from advancing in your career, it will be worth the time it takes to stop and analyze just where you stand in your life's work. Whether you are an attorney, minister, shop supervisor, homemaker, physician, truck driver, or radio announcer, you have certain expectations that you hold for yourself and that your boss or colleagues hold for you. Are you meeting them?

Use the "Career Analysis" questionnaire in this chapter as an aid in helping you evaluate your current career status. If you are not reaching your goals concerning salary, titles, and responsibilities, you will need to direct some of your time toward personal development and additional training.

In this effort, you won't want to waste time by further developing skills you've already perfected. Focus instead on overcoming weaknesses and getting rid of career blind spots. The "Rank and File" lists in this chapter will show you how to determine the areas in your career that need shoring up.

The main thing to remember about developing time-management skills is that you cannot begin any sooner than now. It's time to stop hiding behind clichés such as "time flies" or "there aren't enough hours in the day."

Actually, there are plenty of hours in the day. I can prove it.

Let's suppose that you have a secret ambition to become a novelist or a customized desk craftsman or a gourmet cook. You haven't pursued your dream because, well, there "wasn't enough time." Still, you hope that perhaps someday—

Well, guess what? I now can make your dream come true in just one calendar year. That is, if you **really** want to devote a little time toward realizing your goal, and the best part is that you can keep your regular job, still get plenty of sleep, and not mess up your weekends.

What you need to do is set aside two hours per day, Monday through Friday, to devote to your goal. It will probably mean doing away with coffee klatches, evening television, and some other nonessential activities that you now engage in on a regular basis. But it will be worth it.

Each day has twenty-four hours. You can sleep eight hours, work at your regular job eight hours, and then use six hours for any activities you wish. But save two hours per day, Monday through Friday, for your special project. Don't be afraid to juggle your schedule to meet this challenge: do your project from 6 to 8 A.M. before the family arises or from noon until 2 P.M. when the children are down for a nap or from 9 to 11 P.M. when everyone else is in bed.

Here's what will happen: At the end of one week, you will have spent ten hours working on your special project (5 days X 2 hours per day=10 hours). At the end of one month, you will have logged a regular 40 hour work-week on your project (4 weeks X 10 hours per week=40 hours). At the end of one calendar year, you will have logged three solid months of 40 hour work-weeks on your project (40 hours per month X 12 months=480 hours=3 months).

And let's face it, if you can't rough out a novel or build one desk or learn to cook a gourmet meal after 480 hours of practice, you just aren't trying. For a fact, however, after 480 hours devoted to your project, you will be competent at it. So, get it straight in your mind right from the start: there are enough hours in the day to do whatever you want to do, but you've got to have discipline.

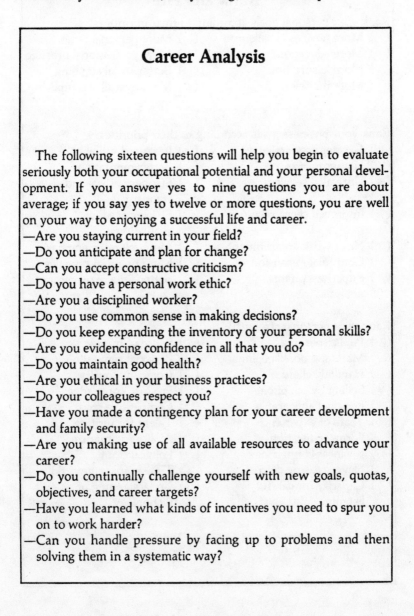

Career Analysis

The following sixteen questions will help you begin to evaluate seriously both your occupational potential and your personal development. If you answer yes to nine questions you are about average; if you say yes to twelve or more questions, you are well on your way to enjoying a successful life and career.

—Are you staying current in your field?
—Do you anticipate and plan for change?
—Can you accept constructive criticism?
—Do you have a personal work ethic?
—Are you a disciplined worker?
—Do you use common sense in making decisions?
—Do you keep expanding the inventory of your personal skills?
—Are you evidencing confidence in all that you do?
—Do you maintain good health?
—Are you ethical in your business practices?
—Do your colleagues respect you?
—Have you made a contingency plan for your career development and family security?
—Are you making use of all available resources to advance your career?
—Do you continually challenge yourself with new goals, quotas, objectives, and career targets?
—Have you learned what kinds of incentives you need to spur you on to work harder?
—Can you handle pressure by facing up to problems and then solving them in a systematic way?

Rank and File

Rank your personal goals according to their priorities:

( ) More business challenges   ( ) More personal fame
( ) More education   ( ) More professional prestige
( ) More leisure time   ( ) Better social standing
( ) More money   ( ) More overall accomplish-
                                     ments

Rank your business goals according to their priorities:

( ) Greater productivity   ( ) Increased visibility
( ) Higher profits   ( ) Better reputation
( ) Unrivaled services   ( ) Stronger ethics and
                                     standards
( ) Improved client relations ( ) Stricter product
                                     evaluations
( ) Nicer work environment   ( ) More scientific emphasis
( ) Continual expansion   ( ) More financial reserves
( ) Superior systems   ( ) Better time management
    analysis

Rank your personal strengths:

( ) Public speaking   ( ) Sense of humor
( ) Math and bookkeeping   ( ) Personal reputation
( ) Handling clients   ( ) Company loyalty
( ) Selling by telephone   ( ) Product knowledge
( ) Personal appearance   ( ) Competitive spirit
( ) Years of experience   ( ) Talent for writing
( ) Formal education   ( ) Ability to organize
( ) Business connections   ( ) Political clout
( ) Never-ceasing drive   ( ) Time management skills
( ) Capacity for careful   ( ) Understanding of
    listening   technology

Part 2:
Beating Clutter and
Procrastination

An old joke relates well to the misconceptions many people today have about time management. It seems that one day a man was driving by an apple orchard when he happened to see a farmer lifting his pigs one at a time up to the tree branches so that the pigs could eat the apples. The man stopped his car, got out, and approached the farmer. "Excuse me," he said, "but isn't that an awfully time-consuming practice?" The farmer looked at the man, shrugged his shoulders, and said, "So what? What's time to a pig?"

Whereas the absurdity of the farmer's situation in our story is evident and obvious, situations that are equally as absurd yet not nearly as obvious exist in countless businesses, churches, and families today. It behooves the time-conscious person to examine his or her time-management practices to make sure they are functional and practical. The greatest desire in the world to be a hard worker is of no value if a person's work is simply wheel spinning rather than forward motion.

To begin with, we must realize that while it's true that all people are given the same number of hours each day, days each week, weeks each month, and so on, it is also true that no two people have the same innate feelings about time. Clocks, schedules, deadlines, calendars, and history books evoke different emotions from different people.

Most of these emotions are conditioned responses; that is, they have been formed in the conscious and subconscious minds of individuals through various experiences. A good experience repeated frequently will develop a good attitude; a bad experience, a bad attitude. This was recently proven when a major company switched payday from Fridays to Mondays. The employees quit saying, "Thank goodness it's Friday" as much as they used to; furthermore, the rate of absenteeism on Mondays was cut by more than 30 percent. People arrived at work smiling on Mondays instead of frowning, mumbling, and groaning.

Knowing this, have you ever tried to analyze why you feel as you do about matters related to time? Give yourself a simple word analysis test. What emotions do you feel when you hear each of these words: **late . . . work . . . pressure . . . deadline . . . interruptions . . . procrastination . . . race . . . waiting . . . stopwatch . . . organized . . . delegating . . . stall . . . schedule . . . system . . . clock.**

You'll discover that your emotional responses regarding words related to time vary greatly. That's not unusual. The fact is, they vary greatly even among individuals who have similar jobs, work schedules, salaries, and social lives. To one person the sound of an alarm clock is similar to a starting gun signaling the chance to get into the day's race, whereas to another person it is like a death knell summoning him or her to the "funeral" of the day's morbid events. To one person, frequent interruptions are reinforcements of the fact that he or she is very important to every activity at the office, whereas to another person they are aggravating, work-stopping frustrations that are not appreciated.

It is important that you realize you do have emotional responses to phases of time and elements of time measurement. Once you identify negative feelings, you can work to reshape them to more positive feelings and behavior. When you identify positive feelings, you can feel confident about them and use them even more directly.

Chapter 5:

Return on the Hour

The most common negative feeling about time that people have is a sense of being **busy** but not very **productive.** Studies have shown that no matter what business a person may be in, he or she falls victim to the "80/20 syndrome." Invariably, 20 percent of what a person does yields 80 percent of his or her net progress and, in correlation, 80 percent of a person's time is usually spent on busywork that produces only 20 percent of the person's total work accomplishments.

The only real way to get more leverage on the 80/20 syndrome is to learn to establish work priorities and then devote time to each item according to its priority rank. Expressed symbolically, don't open an acorn when you could be chopping down an oak tree; don't build model cars when you could be racing in the Indianapolis 500. Establish priority tasks in ranking order. Stay on each task until it is either completed or moved along as far as you can push it for that day. Don't fill your time with numerous "go-fer" jobs when you should be using your time to fulfill a major objective.

You should begin early in the day to work on your top priority items. You accomplish two things by doing this: first, you guarantee that **real** progress will be made each day, and second, you remain in control of things even if interruptions later arise (because your priority items have already been completed or have been well-advanced). You can use the chart in this chapter to learn how to set up your daily tasks by priority rankings.

One thing you will quickly discover once you start devoting your prime time to your prime tasks is that you won't have time to do many of the time filler things you used to handle. At that point, I recommend that you take a few minutes to list many of the things you are in the habit of doing but that are not really related to big projects. For instance, are you sending reminder memos to clients who never miss payments anyway? Are you attending business meetings that really don't relate to your job function? Are you still handling an interim responsibility that you were supposed to have been able to give up half a year ago? If you say yes to these or similar questions, begin to drop those time-wasting habits.

Chapter 6:

Learn to Delegate

One of the best ways to get rid of time filler jobs is to give them to someone else. The more you can delegate, the more you'll be free for bigger tasks. You must ask yourself three questions before deciding to delegate a job: (1) Am I the only person qualified to do this job? (2) Does this job involve anything confidential that I should not be sharing with an assistant? and (3) Will it take me longer to explain how to do the job than it would just to go ahead and do it myself?

Whenever you delegate a task, give specific instructions about what you want done, and set an exact time when you want the job to be completed. Be cautious about the person to whom you choose to delegate a job. Choose someone who is capable, responsible, and productive. As a fail-safe measure, allow for a little time cushion on deadlines whenever you delegate something. After all, your work will never be as important to someone else as it will be to you.

In finance, investors refer to a return on the dollar. In time management we must think about our return on the hour. In short, for every hour devoted to our jobs and lives, we must ask ourselves how much return (as profits, enjoyment, or progress) we are receiving.

*"*Love your work, your husband, and your child. If you wonder when you'll get time to rest, well, you can sleep in your old age.*"*

—Beverly Sills

Chapter 7:

The Paper Mill

A simple way to maximize our return on the hour is to develop concentrated tunnel vision. Whenever you have to work out a problem, clear your desk of everything that does not specifically relate to that problem. This will eliminate distracting clutter and it will allow you to focus on the top priority item until it is completed. As each job is finished, clear off the previous job's reference materials and replace them with the next job's materials (reference books, pamphlets, folders, files). Proceed then as before and keep in control at all times the paper on your desk and around you.

Paper shuffling, you see, has long been recognized as a great time-wasting process. Most people hang on to notes, memos, and reports as though they were running a national archive. That sort of fanaticism is costly in both time and money, and it's completely needless. (Even the IRS sets a routine limit of going back only three years to check a taxpayer's records.)

Some years ago I was working in the public relations department of a small midwestern college. The school fell on rough times at one point and each department was asked to reduce its annual expenditures by 10 percent.

One of the ways the public relations department decided to save funds was to stop photocopying five copies of all reports. Prior to this, each person in the department had been given a copy of each report prepared for study or action. Under the new system a buck slip was to be placed on each report; as the report was read by a staff member, the slip was initialed and the report was passed along to the next person.

This alteration in procedure was expected to cause some time delays, but it might save nearly a thousand dollars annually in photocopy costs. To our surprise, the results were completely **positive:** this change actually saved time, increased productivity, and saved $3,500.

Here's what happened: first, the department secretaries found they had an extra five hours each week to work on priority projects now that they no longer had to go back and forth to the photocopy room to make report copies and then walk from office to office to deliver the copies; second, instead of five separate editings of a report that had to be brought together into one final draft, the reports now arrived at the final person with cummulative editorial comments on the one copy. One retyping completed the job. Third, with 80 percent of all new report files suddenly eva- porating, the department was able to cancel orders for new file cabinets and storage lockers. We had increased productivity, become more time efficient, and saved thousands of dollars simply by doing one thing—getting rid of paper. You can do the same thing. Follow these procedures:

1. **Pitch it whenever possible.** If someone else has a copy on file of a report you're holding, destroy your copy. If it's not a legal document, permanent historical record, or vital resource reference, burn whatever paper you have. Don't retain catalogs—just the pages you need and the order form. Toss all junk mail into the wastebasket as soon as it arrives.

2. **Seek condensed material.** Don't request data, statistics, or reports unless they are vital; if they are needed, get a digest version or a pertinent excerpt from a larger report.

3. **Handle paper just once.** Respond to memos or letters when

they come in. Read reports, pamphlets, or brochures in one sitting.

4. **Rely on short responses.** Never send a letter if you can jot a postcard. Never write a report if you can dictate a memo. Be terse.

5. **Purge your files.** Review your total file system every twenty-four months and discard as much paper as possible. Cancel any suspended-operation files. Eliminate seldom-used reference files. Save time and space by keeping a fast-grab file on your desk that contains frequently called phone numbers, deadline reminders, and lists of projects to brainstorm about before tackling.

Each day, do all you can to fill the wastebasket rather than your file cabinets.

//Ah, but a man's reach should exceed his grasp, or what's a heaven for?**//**

—Robert Browning

Chapter 8:

Stop Stopping

nother time-management problem relates to getting started. Ben Franklin once said, "The two things I hate most about each day's activities are going to bed and getting out of bed." In his own homespun way, Franklin had explained what time and motion experts now refer to as "the power of inertia."

In essence, the power of inertia makes us want to continue to do what we currently **are** doing. If we are resting, we want to stay in bed. If we are working, we want to remain working. Knowing this helps us understand why procrastination is so prevalent in people. Unless workers can force themselves to get started on a job and build up inertia, it remains easier and easier to stay at the current activity. But that's procrastination. And it's the worst habit a person can develop.

Procrastination is a lot like lying. Indulging even a little leads to a bad habit of it, and before long it gets you into serious trouble. Still, no one will deny that not all work is enjoyable and that getting started is often difficult. There are ways of dealing with this problem, however.

Whenever a task seems overwhelming, remember what Henry Ford once said about no job being too difficult to do if it can be broken down into a lot of smaller jobs. That bit of wisdom helped me learn to write books. After many years of working as a newspaper columnist and magazine feature writer, I was asked to write a very long and detailed book about the life and writings of American author Jack London.

Having never written anything longer than three-thousand words, the book on London seemed an awesome task for me. Sensing my apprehension, my publisher said, "Don't think of it as a 325-page book. Think of the fifteen chapters as fifteen individual feature articles on a related topic. When the series of fifteen articles is done, we'll assemble it as a collection. That collection will become the book." With this new perspective, I prepared the fifteen "articles" and a year later my first book was published.

You can follow the same procedure. Whenever a task seems overbearing and awesome, focus only on the first phase of it; complete that phase and then move on to the next phase. This will encourage you as you see something get finished each day. It will give you the motivation you'll need to beat procrastination.

Chapter 9:
An Alphabet of Advice

Procrastination can be conquered. Paper clutter can be eliminated. Your life can be more time-conscious. Anytime you begin to feel differently, reread this chapter and get back on the right track.

A. Instead of punishing yourself for wasting time, give yourself rewards each time you manage your time wisely. Reinforce in a positive way.

B. Learn to say no without feeling guilty. If you are asked to do a job and you know you do not have the time to do it to the best of your ability, say no. You do more damage by doing a half-way job of something than you do by refusing to get involved in the first place.

C. Do away with the open-door policy as much as possible. You need tranquility and uninterrupted time whenever you are concentrating.

D. Avoid meetings whenever possible. If you must have a meeting, prepare a specific agenda ahead of time and stick to it.

E. Game plan your twenty-four-hour segments by filling in a

daily schedule and planner each night before bed. Stick to your game plan each day.

F. Set goals and strive to reach them by specific deadline dates.

G. Learn to listen. Instead of rushing headlong into a project, be professional enough to listen to instructions carefully and to heed the advice of others. Usually, this will improve your work and reduce the number of things that you'll need to do over because of error.

H. Stay healthy. Take vitamins, get regular exercise, eat nutritious foods, control your weight, and get regular medical check ups. Time spent in sickbeds or in hospital wards is wasted time.

I. Return calls just before noon or just before 5 P.M. each day. This will prevent the other person from rambling.

J. Use commuting time to listen to cassette tapes that can teach you a new language, show you how to increase customer good will, motivate you to work harder, or help you study your Bible. Don't simply turn on the car radio each morning and evening.

K. Link errands together. Instead of four trips a day, go out just once and stop at the dry cleaner, library, bank, and pastry shop in succession.

L. Instead of long coffee breaks, take five-minute work pauses. This will refresh you but not give you time to lose your work inertia.

M. Learn from your mistakes and don't repeat them.

N. Anticipate change, prepare for it, and adapt quickly when it comes.

O. Use machines that will save you time if you can afford them: self-dialing phones, hand-held miniature tape recorders, word processors, calculators, and so on.

P. Learn to make a decision—to lead, to follow, or to get out of the way.

Q. Eat light lunches. Heavy midday meals make you sluggish during the afternoon.

R. Keep in mind that short naps provide bonus energy for the body. Lay your head down, clear your mind of all thoughts, breathe evenly, and doze off for a few moments. You'll awake refreshed.

S. Arrange your office furniture so that you can reach your

telephone, wastebasket, in/out trays, typewriter, intercom, and bulletin board without having to stand.

T. Use white noise (the hum of a dehumidifier, an FM radio played low) to subdue external distracting noises.

U. Carry two books with you at all times: one to read when you are caught with time on your hands and one with blank pages so that you can write down any good ideas that you suddenly develop.

V. Remember Parkinson's Law: Work expands to fill the time available for its completion. As such, set deadlines that are challenging.

W. Plan your work and work your plan.

X. Never consider defeat. Concentrate on your strengths, not weaknesses.

Y. Combine tasks whenever possible. Stuff advertisements in envelopes while talking on the phone. Shine your shoes while watching the evening news on TV.

Z. Build some slack time into your daily schedule (one open appointment time, a shorter lunch hour) so that unforeseen interruptions do not cause a panic.

//Keep away from people who try to belittle your ambitions. Small people always do that, but the really great make you feel that you, too, can become great.**//**

—Mark Twain

Part 3:
Time-Management
Procedures

I n our first section of this book we discussed ways in which you could discover what your weak areas in time and life management were. In the second chapter we discovered how you could begin right now (without any further procrastination) to overcome those weaknesses. Now, in this third chapter, we are going to put into practice some procedures that will help you organize yourself better and assist you in running your life more efficiently.

Nine primary procedures serve as the foundation for your time-management plans. They will be discussed in the following nine chapters of Part 3.

❝Your goals for the next year should be written on paper.❞

Chapter 10:

Sign a Time-Management Contract

Whenever you do business with anyone, you have that person sign a contract for the work to be done. In this way, there is no doubt about what exactly is to be accomplished and upon what date it is to be completed.

You need to draw up a contract by and for yourself. Your goals for the next year should be written down on paper. A date for their completion should be fixed. Your name should be signed to the bottom of this agreement as a personal pledge that upon your word of honor these worthy objectives **will** be achieved. This will keep you from getting sidetracked on lesser-important busy-work activities.

As an additional incentive to fulfill your contract obligation, I recommend that you give copies of it to your spouse or business partners or best friends and ask them to challenge you on the appropriate date. This will motivate you to work harder in order not to be embarrassed by any shortcomings.

This chapter contains a model "Time Management Contract" that you can use to help set your yearly goals.

Time Management Contract

I, _____[full name]_____, agree to accomplish each of the following items on or before [target date] and thereby do formally contract myself to these purposes. These goals are challenging, but reasonable, and I accept them willingly.

(A)

(B)

(C)

(D)

(E)

Signed by: _____Date:_____

Instructions:

1. Select five challenging activities that would improve your life or career and list them on the five lines of your contract.

2. Sign and date the contract.

3. Make three copies of your contract and give one each to three close friends or business associates and ask them to challenge you on the appropriate date.

Chapter 11:

Chart a Life Map

I f you are the kind of person who has always said, "Que sera sera, what will be, will be," it is now time for you to drop that attitude. In its place, develop an attitude of, "By the grace of God, my life will amount to something. I will chart my destiny and stay on course."

I once interviewed a fascinating lady named Ella Tuttle Matteson who, on her one-hundredth birthday, decided that she wanted to become a freelance writer. For two years she studied and practiced every lesson she could find on how to become a professional writer. When Ella was 102 years old she became a weekly columnist for the *Clinton Local* newspaper of Clinton, Michigan. I wrote a story about her for *Writer's Digest* (October 1983, pp. 20-21). One year later, at age 103, Ella was selling short stories and articles to national magazines, and I wrote a story on her for *Woman's World* (March 13, 1984, p. 17).

Ella told me that her secret to success was that each decade she set a new major goal for herself. One decade she was a secretary; the next decade she was a nurse (her late husband was a physician);

the next decade she was a leader in community service. This continued until her tenth decade when she became a free-lance writer.

Now, I ask you: what if Ella had never developed long range vision? What if she had "retired" at age 65? What if she had been fatalistic and had refused to believe that she could control her own fate? Both Ella and the world would have been worse off for it. Fortunately, Ella **did** have long-range vision, and it made her a continual success.

You, too, should have long-range goals. By using the "Life Map" found in this chapter you can force yourself to think about what you want your career, financial, and security levels to be during your current years, midlife years, and post-retirement years.

At the bottom of the map, list your life and career achievements thus far. Then fill in the goals you have for a year from now, and three, five, ten, fifteen, and thirty years from now. Put the appropriate future dates next to each goal, too. At the end of the map, use the space at the top to write your own obituary or Who's Who entry. In short, decide today what you will be remembered for having accomplished. Having decided upon that, begin to strive for it.

The "Life Map" is an essential part of your time-management practices. If I put you behind the wheel of a car in New York City, gave you a good map, and told you to drive to Los Angeles, five days later you would arrive there. If I didn't give you a map, you'd meander all over the country for days, months, and years until you finally drove off into the Grand Canyon and we'd never hear from you again.

Life is the same way. Map it out and you'll be able to reach your predetermined destinations. Ignore a map and you'll just wander aimlessly.

Life Map	
RETIREMENT DATE:	(Write a Who's Who entry about your life and accomplishments.)
DATE: MY GOALS:	Thirty Years From Now
DATE: MY GOALS:	Fifteen Years From Now
DATE: MY GOALS:	Ten Years From Now
DATE: MY GOALS:	Five Years From Now

DATE: Three Years
MY GOALS: From Now

DATE: One Year
MY GOALS: From Now

(Write a summary of your professional
accomplishments to date.)

X STARTING POINT

Chapter 12:

Use a Daily
Schedule And Planner

All efficient managers of time are list makers. Some fill out to-do lists, others jot notes on desk calendars, and still others use daybooks or office planners. I use a daily schedule and planner as shown in the example in this chapter. It reminds me of my short- and long-range goals, it keeps my life priorities in order, and it serves as my memory for daily-action items. You may wish to modify the listed categories to fit your particular needs. The main goal is to get into the habit of writing plans down.

A list helps you three ways. First, it frees your mind to be more creative and receptive to new ideas because you won't have to hold important items in your memory. Second, a list lets you make use of ten minutes before lunch to make a phone call or fifteen minutes before the day's end to dictate a quick letter because all your action items are before you at a glance. Thus, you can use all your little pockets of time. Third, as you review the list at the end of each day and see dozens of crossed-out accomplished items, you'll feel like a winner and will be eager to continue your success when tomorrow comes.

Daily Schedule and Planner

Today's Date:_____

This Week's Goal:_____

This Month's Goal:_____

This Year's Project:_____

MY LIFE PRIORITIES:	TODAY'S ERRANDS:	PEOPLE TO SEE TODAY:
	FAMILY MATTERS TO ATTEND TO:	

PHONE CALLS TO MAKE:	LETTERS TO WRITE:	READING/ RESEARCH PROJECTS:	MISC.
APPOINT- MENTS AND SCHEDULED INTER- VIEWS:	TYPING TO DO:		

Chapter 13:

Link Your Tasks Together

As you set out to accomplish all you have written on your Daily Schedule and Planner, take an ink pen and link those tasks unrelated to your salaried work that can be done either in rapid succession or simultaneously.

Let's say that under **appointments** you have written "see Mrs. Davis at 12:30 P.M. to deliver property deed." Under **errands,** you have written "pick up cake for secretary's office birthday party tomorrow" and "see Billy's teacher at elementary school for conference at 1 P.M." You also have a reminder note to "see reference librarian at public library about books on dress-for-success." And you see that your spouse has jotted down "drop off suits at cleaners."

Instead of leaving your home or office five times during the day, you should arrange for these five tasks to be done in rapid succession during one trip. You can leave at noon and pick up the cake at the bakery and drop off your suits at the cleaners on your way to see Mrs. Davis at 12:30. After a ten-minute visit with her, you can stop briefly at the library to pick up the books you called ahead for and then go to the elementary school for your 1 P.M. meeting with your son's teacher. By 1:45 you can be back where you started.

A day that has a 9 A.M. trip to the bakery, a 10:30 A.M. run to the cleaners and library, a 12:30 P.M. visit to a client, and a 1 P.M. trip to a school is a day that has wasted at least ninety minutes in needless travel time. By linking tasks and errands, you can stay on a schedule, accomplish more, and also save yourself some gasoline expense.

You should also think of ways to do simultaneous work. If you have to stuff envelopes with a monthly newsletter, do so while you are talking on the telephone. If your shoes need shining, buff them up while you are dictating letters into a tape recorder. If there are articles in one of your professional magazines that you need to read, do so while you are having the stylist cut your hair. **Always keep in mind that the key to good time management is not to work harder, but to work smarter.**

Chapter 14:

Set and Follow Deadlines

T o be efficient at time management, you must get into the habit of setting and following self-imposed deadlines. Each day you should evaluate how much time you will need to complete a project and then see to it that you finish by or before the end of that time period.

I used to work as a newspaper reporter for The *Muncie Star*. In that line work, the word **deadline** was a literal term. It meant, "Go past this line, and you're dead." If you missed your deadline, you also missed your byline and your salary and your next assignment. So, I learned early in life to respect deadlines.

Don't be overly generous when establishing your deadline dates for yourself. Parkinson's Law states, "Work expands in accordance to the time allotted to accomplish it." That means that if you give yourself two days in which to prepare a sales presentation, you will have it ready in two days; however, if you give yourself four days in which to prepare it, you probably will take the full four days. So don't be afraid to tighten the time girth a bit when setting deadlines.

Finishing ahead of a deadline is a display of excellent time-management skills. You know how it is with bank loans: pay off the loan one month ahead of time and you will earn yourself an A-1 credit rating; pay off the loan one month behind time and you will be labeled a bad-risk borrower. The same goes for work. If you have promised a client that a certain job will be completed by next Monday and then you call the client and announce you'll have it ready three days early, you will make a very favorable impression on that client. So strive to "beat the clock."

Chapter 15:

Learn to Make Decisions

Stephen R. Leimberg wrote an impressive statement: "Learn how to make a decision—to lead, to follow, or to get out of the way. Typically, it costs far more to procrastinate and do nothing than it does to make your move and accept your occasional mistakes."

Leimberg is right. Not to decide is to decide. Stalling, delaying, and procrastinating are not the techniques used in good time management. Instead, you must analyze the data before you, weigh the options, then come to a decision. The fact of the matter is, some things are more important than others and a decision must be made to make those items a top priority. For assistance in learning how to do this, study the "Focusing on Priorities" chart found on page 51.

You can develop specific habits that will help you become a better decision maker. When letters and other items of mail come to you, give an immediate response to them by phone or return mail or inter-office memo. When people suggest you should attend or call a meeting, decide right then if it would warrant the time it would involve; if not, say no. When your secretary tells you of some crisis ("I've accidentally booked two different appointments for you at the same time this afternoon"), consider a wise solution and put it into immediate action to alleviate the crisis.

While it is true that snap decisions are seldom productive, it is also true that your first response after taking a moment to weigh options is usually your best response. So, if pressed for time, go with it, and don't get bogged down in how-will-this-turn-out worries.

Chapter 16:

Tap Your Biorhythm Peak

I n recent years scientists have given us results of biorhythm studies to prove to us something we knew all along: different people work best at varied times of the day.

My father and I are good examples of this difference. My father grew up on a farm where the workday began at 5 A.M. This didn't bother him. He enjoys being up when the air is a little crisp, the sun is not glaring yet, and the strength of a good night's rest is in his body.

My father is a successful businessperson. He owns three companies. Nevertheless, he still goes to his office around 6:30 A.M. each morning. He has dictated half-a-dozen letters onto a tape recorder by the time his secretaries arrive at 8 A.M. He doesn't have to get up that early; he just likes to. He says his mind is keenest when he first wakes up.

Now me, I'm just the opposite. I hate mornings. When I get up, I don't talk, I don't smile, and I don't move very quickly. In college I had to attend several 8 A.M. classes, and during my stint in the army my day began at 6 A.M. I never got used to early mornings and I never liked them. I don't even become civilized until 10 A.M. or later.

I am one of those persons who comes alive at night. I love the nights. When the TV set is turned off, the kids are put in bed, the movement and noises outdoors cease, and the blackness of night hides all ancillary distractions, I turn on. I go to my home office, pick up a pencil and some paper, and begin to write. From 10 P.M. until 2 A.M. I am at my creative peak. No one disturbs me, nothing interrupts me. My production output is impressive.

My father's prime working time is early morning; my prime time is late at night. We each have successful careers because we have developed our work habits to accommodate our peak biorhythm times. While my father is in bed sawing logs, I'm in my office writing an involved short story or outlining the chapters for my next business book. By the time I am finally in bed and dozing off, my father is probably awake and standing in front of a mirror shaving and whistling.

To tap into the power of your prime time, ask yourself which two consecutive hours you enjoy most each day and feel your best. Is it 7 to 9 A.M.? noon until 2 P.M.? 10 P.M. until midnight? Having made this decision, structure your work efforts so that your most important challenges will face you then. **Do not use prime time hours for reading the newspaper, making phone calls, or watching television.** Use these hours to plan a new business venture, redesign your home or office, dictate important letters or contracts, visit clients, or whatever else may be of major importance to your life or career.

Part of good time-management practices calls for an analysis of the quality of the various hours of your day. You should use your **prime time** for your **prime tasks.**

It is important that you learn to spend your prime time on your prime tasks. It is also important that you learn to take one job at a time and to stay with it until it is complete (or moved along as far as it can go at this time). The chart "Focusing on Priorities" will help you focus on the jobs that really merit and need your priority attention.

Focusing on Priorities			
	Item	Deadline	Related Factors
Crucial Item			
Priority Item			
Especially Important Item			
Important Item			
Accountable Item			
Functional Item			
Routine Item			

"Determine never to be idle. It is wonderful how much may be done if we are always doing."

—Thomas Jefferson

Chapter 17:

Wheel Spinners or Time Managers

Being able to decide which tasks you should tackle personally and which tasks you should delegate to others is as important a time management decision as you are ever likely to make. If you pass along work to a competent person who can get the job done right, you will save yourself hours of time. If you pass along a job to just anyone who happens to be available and the work becomes disorganized and improperly carried out, you can create a double workload for yourself later when you have to step in to straighten things out.

When you delegate work, choose the right person. This will not necessarily be the secretary or subordinate at your office who gives the appearance of being a workaholic. Compulsive workers might appear to be perfect employees because they work long hours, sometimes day and night. But the hours these overly zealous workers put in often do not equal the work they produce. They aren't necessarily efficient. They may rush around helter-skelter, constantly jotting memos or placing phone calls, but many times the tasks they do aren't necessary. They have lost sight of the real purpose of their work. So keep in mind that there's a difference between a productive worker and a wheelspinner and delegate your work to competent time managers.

Knowing when to delegate something can be determined by asking yourself three quick questions: (1) Can this task be delegated, or am I the only person qualified to do it properly? (2) If I delegate this task, will it take me longer to explain what needs to be done than it would take for me just to do it myself? (3) Does this task involve anything confidential that I should not bring someone else in on?

Basically, a good time manager will delegate all routine or mundane specific tasks (opening the mail, answering the phone, updating files, cleaning the office) to people whose time costs the agency or parent chain operation less than his or hers does. Specific instructions and an expected completion time should be given with each delegated task. The "Save Time by Delegating" chart on page 55 will show you how to do this.

Once you delegate a task, don't oversupervise it. Instead, expect proper progress and good results. An occasional review is never out of line, however. Don't let a delegated task be postponed; occasionally ask how the project is coming along and encourage your subordinate to stay on schedule. Never let a delegated task be handed back to you unfinished; permit this to happen once and you will set a precedent you cannot overcome.

Save Time by Delegating

Are you doing work you should be delegating to others? Each time you teach someone else to do a job, you free yourself from that task and provide more time for your more important work.

Think of four routine tasks you now do regularly that you could delegate to someone else:

	Item	Frequency
1.		
2.		
3.		
4.		
5.		
6.		

Now, prepare a specific plan for delegating these four routine jobs to someone else:

	Task	To Be Delegated To:	In This Way:
1.			
2.			
3.			
4.			
5.			
6.			

Chapter 18:

Relax Constructively

Any competent shop supervisor will tell you that machines need periodic rests ("cool down time") and regular maintenance. The human body is much the same way. We need to get proper exercise, eat a balanced diet, enjoy moments of laughter, accept offerings of praise and love from friends and family members, and indulge in some quiet time alone or change-of-pace activities with companions. Such things keep us mentally balanced and physically healthy. None of us qualify as cloistered monks or galley slaves who have but one twenty-four-hour-a-day life objective.

There's nothing wrong with relaxation. We all need it. But even in our times of relaxation we can be conscious of the preciousness of time and we can show respect for it. In so doing, we can relax constructively by taking a healthy walk, reading a book, writing letters to our friends, or spending quality time with our children. Weekly hours wasted on coffee breaks or spent in needless rambling conversations on the telephone or squandered in front of the television set watching anything that comes on are seldom constructive or really relaxing. You can do better. It's your time: value it!

Six days you shall labor and do all your work, but the seventh day is a Sabbath to the Lord your God. On it you shall not do any work.

—Exodus 20:8-10

Part 4:
Eliminating
Duplication Work

One of the classic questions of life is, Why is there never enough time to do it right the first time, but always enough time to do it over after you've messed it up? Phrased more euphemistically, The hurrieder I go, the behinder I get.

In this chapter we are going to learn how to save countless numbers of hours by mastering techniques that will enable us to do things as they should be done the first time. By eliminating duplication work we can always be advancing to newer and more fascinating duties and assignments.

"Quality control is a key factor in good time management."

Chapter 19:

Do It Right

I t is always more time efficient and less costly to do tasks correctly the first time. Many people who punch out a business contract or zip through a sales presentation or bang out an idea think that they are really saving time. They are only deceiving themselves, however. Poor quality work and poor service are negative factors in personal time management.

If you race through a sales presentation so quickly that a client has to make two follow-up phone calls to you, you haven't saved time. If you hastily dictate a letter and "save time" by not proofreading it before it goes out, you will lose time when a client calls to ask about missing information.

Quality control is a key factor in good time management. The fewer the number of things you have to redo, the more time you will save.

You can become wealthy by preventing mistakes and errors. There is absolutely no excuse for having errors in the materials you are responsible for or mistakes in the services you provide. Should you package your materials any less skillfully than a parachute packer packages hers? Should you operate any less skillfully than a brain surgeon operates?

Errors spin off more errors, and the lack of a systematic way of controlling them compounds your problems. You must confront errors openly, not abusing any person who caused an error but instead doing something to guarantee that the system that permitted the error gets changed. Keep the pressure on to prevent errors. Get into the habit of doing tasks right the first time. Remember: your job is not to **detect** errors (that's duplicating your work) but to **prevent** errors from occurring in the first place.

Here are the four most common reasons for a lack of quality control:

• **A lack of attention:** you are too tired, too bored, or too restless to pay attention to what you're doing.

• **A lack of desire:** because of a physical illness or a form of mental stress or perhaps a lack of proper incentives, you have no desire to do what you've been told to do.

• **A poor attitude:** you are willing to accept mediocrity. Thus, you'll never strive for perfection in what you do.

• **A refusal to accept instruction:** you are too proud, too busy, or too unconcerned to take the time to learn new and better ways of upgrading your work.

You can insure quality control by following these tips:

• **Set high standards** for the work you do and see to it that everyone working with you understands the necessity of having such standards.

• **Conduct periodic** in-depth **reviews** of work being done for you (everything from the typing your secretary does to the office cleaning your janitorial service provides), and be certain people do not relax the standards you have set.

• Remember that quality service is both a business and an **ethical** standard in all businesses;

• **Get adequate rest,** vary your daily routine, and take pride in your work.

• **Never take things for granted.**

Quality is nothing more than **conformance to requirements,** notes expert Philip Crosby. It can be measured exactly. The laws of nature do not allow for a margin of error and neither should the laws of good business. Quality work is time-saving and cost-saving work. Nonconformance to quality results in extra work hours and extra pay-out hours.

When you do something, do it right or don't do it at all.

═══

Dost thou love Life? Then do not squander Time; for that's the stuff life is made of.
—Benjamin Franklin

═══

Chapter 20:

Reduce Your Interruptions

One of the prime reasons you duplicate much of your work is because you frequently get interrupted and later have to start all over again at what you had previously been doing.

Unexpected interruptions are the worst sappers of any worker's daily time. For that reason, they need to be controlled as much as possible. In doing so, you may have to go against some of your established thinking; in the long run, however, it will do wonders for your personal and professional lives (not to mention your sanity). Here are six basic tips on how to reduce the number of interruptions you face in life:

First, learn how to say no without feeling guilty about it. If you are too busy at present to serve on a committee, say so. If your goals are going to keep you too occupied to accept an offer to bowl or golf on a league this summer, make your apologies to your teammates and bow out for a season. Keep your goals and life priorities in mind and don't be ashamed to protect the time needed for them by saying no to ancillary activities.

Second, abandon the all-day-long open-door policy. Secure a block of private time for yourself each day (at least one solid hour and two if you can manage it). Do not allow anyone to interrupt you for any reason. Unhook the phone; put up a "Do Not Disturb" sign; station your secretary outside your door as a guard; go hide in your church's library —do anything you have to in order to protect that time period. You need uninterrupted time to do serious thinking, tackle big jobs, or work on special plans; so, build this time slot into your daily schedule.

Third, exert more control over your working environment. If people walking by in the hall distract you, close your door. If your secretary's electric pencil sharpener breaks your train of thought, ask her or him not to run it while you are doing paperwork. If mumbled conversations in adjoining offices or rooms at home annoy you, use the drone of a dehumidifier as white noise or an FM radio for a counter-noise override. If the interior decorating in your office is brassy and annoying, change it. Your ability to be a successful worker is of foremost importance; let everything else be subordinated to that objective.

Fourth, assemble all your supplies before you begin a project. Leaving your work area every ten minutes to get files, records, charts, reference books, thumbtacks, staples, notepads, typing paper, or whatever supplies your project calls for will not only waste valuable time, but it will also continually break your train of thought and disrupt the intense concentration you need to devote to the project at hand. So, assemble your materials before you begin an important project, and show the same seriousness a general shows when planning the logistics of a battle campaign. The Boy Scout motto is still a good piece of advice: **be prepared.**

Fifth, plan for a work pause. Most people feel they need a half-hour coffee break in the morning and afternoon. Nonsense. That is twenty wasted hours per month. Instead, give yourself occasional five-minute breaks for deepbreathing exercises, a slow-munching nutritional snack, a brisk walk outside, or a few moments of relaxed daydreaming. A brief breather usually serves as an adequate change of pace for regenerating the creative thought processes and revitalizing the work motive, but it doesn't distract you long enough to make you forget about where you were in your project.

Sixth, build a little slack time into your daily routine. The inevitable interruption must be recognized as a reality. So, when it occurs, handle it and then get back on schedule. If you have allowed some flex-time (a shorter lunch hour, an open appointment time each day, some overrun time at the day's end), you won't panic over having been thrown out of synchronization with your planned events of the day.

The basic lesson here is that interruptions are saboteurs of good time-management practices. They must be guarded against, controlled, or eliminated. If termites were eating away at your house, you would exterminate them. If interruptions are eating away at your time-management efforts, you must eliminate them. Schedules and systems are like hot-air balloons: keep them intact and they will fly; poke holes in them and they will never get off the ground.

If you are in business, provide your secretary with three lists of people and some instructions on how to screen their calls. The first list will pinpoint people you will talk to anytime they phone you, such as your district supervisor, prospects calling to set up appointment times, your spouse, or executives from your company's home office.

The second list will note people whom you will talk to during normal office hours but not when you are concentrating on a special project or in a conference with someone; these people may include service club presidents, certain relatives, or your business colleagues.

The third list will focus on people you do not wish to talk to (you can call them back if it's important), such as politicians seeking donations, long-winded friends, office furniture salespeople, people wanting to know if you need a part-time employee for summer, or radio quiz show disc jockeys who call numbers at random. Your secretary can serve as a sieve; only the important, business-related calls should reach you.

Next, you should learn to set the tone when you want phone calls to be brief. Saying, "What can I do for you?" is more effective than is a time-consuming pleasantry such as, "It's good to hear from you again." Be courteous, but keep the conversation in line with its purpose. Get off the phone as soon as possible. If necessary, buy a three-minute egg timer and turn it over when your phone rings. When the sand runs out, make an effort to end the conversation. If you find it difficult to end conversations, you might consider having a telephone amplifier installed in your office or home so that you can be working at your file cabinet or retrieving things from your cupboards while you are still talking.

Finally, reduce incoming phone calls by initiating necessary calls yourself and getting them behind you for the day. The outline of "When to Call" shown in our chart in this chapter will help you to target your calls for maximum effectiveness. Also, get into the habit of suggesting specific times when people should return calls to you. Say, "Why don't you call me tomorrow morning at 9:30 with your answer?" or "I'll expect to hear from you after 4 P.M. tomorrow, all right?" This will put people on your schedule and not vice versa.

Chapter 21:

Manage the Telephone

Have you ever been on one of those telephone merry-go-rounds of, "You call me back after you talk to Bob, then I'll talk to Mary so that she can call you back about what Fred decides to call me about?"

It gets crazy, doesn't it? You spend an hour on the phone trying to get ten related messages coordinated into one answer. You need more control over your phone than that.

The telephone can be your best friend or your worst enemy, depending on how you use it. Used as a technical tool able to save steps, trips, and time, it is your best friend. Used as a chatterbox time-killer, it is your worst enemy.

Many people pride themselves on having a gift for gab. If you are a peddler pulling a wagon from farm to farm, that's fine. But if you are a time-conscious individual, you need to be more in control of your conversations. Nowhere is this more applicable than in using the telephone properly. So let's review a few steps that can help you manage your time on the telephone.

When To Phone

To make time-effective use of your telephone, use the following chart to call people at the most convenient times for you to reach them.

Accountants	April 16 to December 31
Attorneys	11 A.M.-2 P.M.; 4-5 P.M.
Bankers	Before 10 A.M.; after 3 P.M.
Builders	Before 8 A.M.; after 5 P.M.
Business Owners	Between 10:30 A.M. and 3 P.M.
Clergy	Between Tuesday and Friday
Dentists	Between 8:30 and 9:30 A.M.
Druggists	Between 1 and 3 P.M.
Engineers and Chemists	Between 4 and 5 P.M.
Executives	After 10:30 A.M.
Homemakers	Midmorning; Midafternoon
Manufacturers	Between 10:30 A.M. and 3 P.M.
Physicians	Before 9:30 A.M.; after 4:30 P.M.
Retail Merchants	Between 1 and 3 P.M.
Sales Managers	Afternoons
Salespeople	Weekends and rainy days
Stockbrokers	Before 10 A.M.; after 3 P.M.
Professors and Teachers	After 4:30 P.M. on weekdays
	Anytime on weekends or holidays

Working customs in your locality may
vary the previously suggested times.

Chapter 22:

Time-effective Appointment Making

I f as a salesperson or the PTA chairperson or a reporter or an insurance agent you need to set up regular appointments with people, follow these guidelines:

• Make your **first** appointment as early as possible each day (a breakfast meeting, if possible) so that you'll have the needed motivation to get up and going each morning.

• Either telephone a reminder or mail out a confirmation card to insure that the appointment will be kept.

• Arrive a little early for the appointment so that you can be comfortable and relaxed when the other party arrives.

――――――――――――――――――――――――――

"A motive is an urge within an individual that incites him or her to action. It is the hope or other force that moves the individual to produce specific results."

—W. Clement Stone

――――――――――――――――――――――――――

Chapter 23:

Listen Carefully

I f you sometimes find that you have to write, call, or visit
someone in order to have that person repeat some information to you, you are duplicating your workload. The way to
avoid this is to become an effective listener. If you hear the
message correctly the first time and retain the important aspects
of it, you won't have to waste valuable time later on by having to
recheck your original contact person for a memory jog.

Here are some tips on how to be an effective listener:

• **Maintain good eye contact.** People want (and deserve) your
undivided attention. Don't glance at TV or thumb through a magazine or play with your pocket calculator when someone is talking
business with you.

• **Use positive body language.** Sit near the speaker; lean slightly
forward to indicate sincere interest; occasionally nod your head
affirmatively.

• **Keep your mind on the topic.** Don't try to anticipate the speaker's remarks. Don't daydream. Don't work hard at coming up with
clever remarks.

• **Take notes.** If you write it down you'll impress the speaker and you'll create a reminder for yourself of what you are supposed to do.

• **Use silence effectively.** Short lulls give the impression you are really weighing what is being said—which you *should* be.

• **Observe common courtesy.** Don't cut people off in the middle of their sentences. Don't echo people by talking along with them. Don't put words in people's mouths; let them tell it in their own way at their own speed.

In this chapter we've seen how quality control, reduced interruptions, telephone control, and effective listening can prevent you from wasting time by duplicating your work actions. Anytime you have a sense of déjà vu—"Haven't I already done part of this job?"—discover immediately what is causing you to repeat your efforts. Eliminate that problem so that you can do things *once* and then move on.

Part 5
On-the-Spot
Time Saving Tips

A drill sergeant once found a scared recruit hiding behind a shrub. When the sergeant demanded to know what the young trooper was doing there, the soldier shrugged his shoulders and replied, "Well, everybody's gotta be someplace."

That's true. What is also true is that no matter where you are—in your car, at the airport, at the office, at home or in a meeting—you can use your time effectively if you plan ahead. Let's see how it's done.

Chapter 24:

Car, Home, and Airport

Keep a cassette tape recorder in your car. You can buy an adapter so that you can run it off current from the cigarette lighter and, thus, not need batteries. In your glove compartment keep a supply of blank tapes.

Whenever you are driving, dictate business letters and other instructions for your secretary. Also use the tapes to record your ideas for an up-coming sales presentation or a special meeting.

Keep some prerecorded tapes in the car that you can listen to while driving. If you need to memorize a speech, read it onto a cassette tape and then play it over and over for yourself while you are driving. If you own a series of tapes that are motivational in nature, keep one or two handy for an emotional lift.

Brainstorming can also be accomplished while driving. If you have a thirty-minute or longer drive ahead of you, jot down five key words in bold print and then tape the paper to the right side of your dashboard. Each time you stop for a railroad crossing or a red light, glance over at the paper and run the words over in your mind: REVIEW ... PERSONAL ... STRENGTHS ... WEAK-

NESSES . . . SUGGESTIONS. Then, as you drive along, concentrate on your abilities as a business person, your strengths and weaknesses, and suggestions or ideas that can better help you meet your goals.

•   •   •

You need to be aware of the difference between **quality** and **quantity** time spent at home. It is not so much a matter of how much time you spend with your family members; it is, instead, a matter of how you use that time.

For example, if you spend three hours in your easy chair watching television while your daughter is sitting on a couch five feet away from you also watching television, that may seem like a lot of time together. In a few days, however, your daughter will never remember anything about that night. If, instead, you had spent just one hour at the kitchen table helping her complete a Girl Scout project for a merit badge, she would remember that forever.

•   •   •

Always **assume** that when traveling by air you will have delays and layovers. In this way, you'll be prepared. Whenever you find yourself with a two- or three-hour layover, make use of the time in these ways:

• **Do Tasks.** Get a haircut; rent a car for your next town; buy gifts to take home to the kids; get your shoes shined.

• **Draft a Business Letter in Longhand.** You can ask your secretary to type it when you get back to the office.

• **Call Clients.** A long-distance phone call has an impact on people. Not only are they impressed, but they are also more apt to get to the point of what you need to discuss.

• **Memorize a Speech.** The concentration needed to make a good speech before a large group can be exercised by mentally practicing the speech while in a noisy terminal.

• **Review Promotional Brochures.** Go through business catalogs. Tear out the pages that interest you and clip them to the order blank. Then throw the rest of the catalog away.

• **Clean Out Your Wallet/Purse.** Throw away gum wrappers, ticket stubs, and business cards of people you never call. Rearrange family photos so that the most recent ones are up front.

Chapter 25:

Meetings, Offices, and Waiting Rooms

Never call a meeting unless there's no other alternative. Invite only those persons who are directly related to the topic of discussion. Prepare an agenda for the meeting and distribute it a day in advance so that committee people can know which reports to bring with them. Announce in advance what time the meeting will end.

Start the meeting on time. Do not backtrack or review for people who arrive late. Tell your secretary to hold all calls. Arrange the meeting room so that chairs are turned away from windows or other possible distractions. Set the room temperature for a comfortable 69°F.

Review the discussions of the previous meetings, if applicable, and make sure that everyone is introduced to each other. Move right into the business for which the meeting was called. Focus on the who, what, when, where, why, how, and how-much aspects of the problem at hand. Attempt to come up with specific solutions or recommendations. End the meeting by reviewing the decisions you've made. Clean up the room before you leave.

After the meeting, send a copy of the minutes to those who attended and those who were absent. At the bottom, note the date, time, and place of the next meeting.

An office is to be functional first, stylish second. In arranging furniture, think about how you work. If you have poor eyesight, move your desk near the natural light of a window. If you make regular references to files, move the file cabinet into the corner nearest your desk and turn it so that the drawers open toward you. Select a desk chair on coasters so that you can roll quickly to the typing stand, file cabinet, or desk rather than always having to stand up and walk away. Keep your wastebasket to your right and slightly behind your chair so that you can drop—not have to throw—things into it.

On a rack or shelf near your phone you should have a row of special reference books (a dictionary, a telephone book, rate books, a road atlas, and so forth.)

Your desk should be free of clutter. You'll need two trays for in and out work (or, as we used to say in the army, "Incoming" and "Retaliation"). Your stapler, tape dispenser, and scissors should be lined up next to the trays.

Your desk phone should be out of your way but at arm's length to your left. By the way, intercoms save steps and are worth the money it costs to install them. Taped to your phone should be a list of **fast jobs** that can be tackled when you find yourself with a few moments on hand before a client shows up for an appointment. (Suggestions: reload the stapler and/or tape dispenser; sharpen pencils; check client files for proper alphabetizing; fill out a requisition form.)

In your upright file folder, keep one folder that contains a list of problems that need special thought and consideration. Whenever you have a canceled appointment or some other unexpected block of free time, reach for this folder and use the time for brainstorming and planning. You will be able to overcome even your biggest problems and challenges if you concentrate on a small portion of them at a time.

• • •

Waiting rooms are appropriately named. That's exactly what visitors are meant to do in them. But you have no time to **wait** for things to happen; you are a person who uses time effectively to **make** things happen. So let's rename waiting rooms. Let's call them **strategy** rooms.

To begin with, you should never wait more than twenty minutes to be shown in to see anyone. (With an abundance of twenty-four-hour medical clinic services in most major towns, this rule applies even to the doctors and dentists you patronize.)

If you are a salesperson and your appointment was scheduled for 10 A.M. and you are not in to see the prospect by 10:20 A.M., inform the receptionist, "I'm terribly sorry, but I will not have enough time now to properly present my program to Ms. Williams. I'll be too pressed to make my 11:30 appointment with another client. Can you set me up for this same time on Thursday or next Monday?" It's a good strategy to show that you are busy, in demand, needed. Successful people like to deal with other successful people. Act successful.

Even the twenty minutes you do wait should be used wisely. In your briefcase, carry company reports to study, business books to read, a pocket calculator for figuring, and a research folder to review about your new prospects. Don't just sit twiddling your thumbs. Use your time.

Becoming Self-Motivated

1. Become aware of what your true desires are.
2. Become determined to obtain those desires.
3. Become disciplined in pursuing those desires.
4. Become enthusiastic and optimistic about your achievements.
5. Become opportunity-oriented.
6. Become confident by becoming knowledgeable in your field.
7. Become the successful person you've dreamed of becoming.

Summary

Time management is like money management: you cannot start it too soon, and **anything** you do is better than doing nothing.

Though concise, this guide has provided you with dozens of pragmatic moves to make and procedures to follow in getting your life organized. If you master all the techniques and ideas found herein and wish to continue your time management studies, a list of references is included at the end of this book.

I wish you well! The clock is running. The rest of your life begins right now. Make it count for something.

Time Management Notes

Suggested Readings on Time Management

Bennett, Arnold. *How To Live on 24 Hours a Day.* New York: Cornerstone Library, 1962.

Bliss, Edwin C. *Getting Things Done.* New York: Bantam Books, 1980.

Brooks, Earl. "Get More Done—Easier," *Nation's Business.* July 1962, 254-56.

Doyle, Michael and David Straus. *How to Make Meetings Work.* New York: Wyden Books, 1976.

Drucker, Peter F. *The Effective Executive.* New York: Harper and Row, 1967.

Engstrom, Ted W. and Alex R. MacKenzie. *Managing Your Time: Practical Guidelines on the Effective Use of Time.* Grand Rapids, Mich.: Zondervan Publishing House, 1967.

Hensley, Dennis E. *Positive Workaholism.* Chicago: R & R Newkirk Co., 1983.

Hensley, Dennis E. *Staying Ahead of Time.* Chicago: R & R Newkirk Co., 1981.

Jones, Curtis H. "The Money Value of Time," *Harvard Business Review.* July-August 1968, 94-101.

Lakein, Alan. *How to Get Control of Your Time and Your Life.* New York: Peter E. Wyden Publishers, Inc., 1973.

Laney, W. L. *How to Be Boss in a Hurry.* Indianapolis: Bobbs-Merrill, 1982.

Lobingier, John L., Jr. *Business Meetings That Make Business.* Toronto, Canada: Collier-MacMillan Limited, 1969.

Machlowitz, Marilyn. *Workaholics.* New York: Mentor Executive Library, 1980.

MacKenzie, R. Alex. *The Time Trap.* New York: AMACON, 1972.

McCay, James R. *The Management of Time.* Englewood Cliffs, N.J.: Prentice-Hall, 1959.

Myers, Robert. "Staying an Hour Ahead—Advantages for Pacific Coast Year Around Daylight Savings," *PSA Magazine.* October 1973, 42-45.

Parkinson, C. Northcote. *Parkinson's Law.* Boston: Houghton-Mifflin, 1957.

Scott, Dru. *How to Put More Time in Your Life.* New York: Signet Books, 1980.

Still, Henry. *Of Time, Tides, and Inner Clocks.* Harrisburg, Pa.: Stackpole Books, 1972.

Terry, George R. *Supervision.* Homewood, Ill.: Richard D. Irving, Inc., 1978.

Trickett, Joseph M. "More Effective Use of Time," *California Management Review.* Summer 1962.

Uris, Auren. "Make Your Time More Productive," *Nation's Business.* May 1962, 58-60.

Webber, Ross A. *Time and Management.* New York: Van Nostrand Reinhold Co., 1972.

86

Time Managment Notes